Traditional Breton Dance Tunes

"Fest Breizh"

50 Traditional Dance Tunes From Brittany

Compiled and Edited by David Surette

Page 2 Drawing by Isa Burke

Music Engraving by Ken Godel

Fest Breizh

Introduction

I have very vivid memories of my first trip into Brittany. I was in my junior year of college, spring of '84, making a long bike trip from my apartment in Dijon west along the Loire Valley and into Brittany. The first day in Brittany I ended up heading for a youth hostel in St. Vincent, alongside the Oust River. The hostel manager was a bearded Celt with a disdain for the French and a passion for Celtic culture, history, music and mythology. One of my only companions at the hostel was a bagpiper from Montréal, Robert Amyot, who had traveled to Brittany to learn more about its musical traditions. Over several bottles of wine at dinner, I sat in rapt attention, spellbound as they traded old stories and invented new ones. The *aubergiste* then set out some single-malt scotch, and the evening continued in similar head-spinning fashion.

That first evening seemed to set the tone for the trip, and indeed sowed seeds that were to blossom into a passion for the music and the culture of Brittany. With my head full of myths and tales (not to mention a bit of a hangover from all those liquid libations) off I biked. I saw standing stones and lovely beaches, old walled towns and Celtic crosses and calvarys. The music was everywhere, but it hit me hardest on one of the last nights of the trip. I was in St. Malo, the old pirate stronghold, and went to a concert featuring a well-known Breton folksinger, Gilles Servat. What really transfixed me was the opening act, a relatively new band called Kornog. This was the musical equivalent of the head-spinning tales of the first night. The tunes wound their way sinuously around each other, the melodies carried on the fiddle, flute and occasional bombarde, while the accompaniments were just as striking, as the guitar and bouzouki wove a spell of ringing, droning strings.

I returned home that summer and tracked down Kornog's first record, *Premiere*. I also started to take note of other Breton tunes nestled here and there among the LPs of the "British Isles" section of my collection (this was before the term "Celtic" became so ubiquitous): a guitar medley by Pierre Bensusan, a dance medley by John Renbourn's group, and a great set of tunes from fiddler Kevin Burke. However, it was not easy to track down a lot of information in those pre-web days, nor was it easy to find other folks who were interested in or experienced with playing Breton tunes. By contrast, it seemed there were loads of folks playing Irish tunes and French-Canadian tunes.

6

I persevered, and this interest eventually led to three return trips to Brittany, with increasing musical involvement each time. Visits to festivals, concerts, dances and music shops led to a travel grant to focus on the music, as well as a writing assignment to spotlight the guitar in Brittany (the *Acoustic Guitar* article from this trip is reproduced in this book). The third trip was actually a solo tour, where I had the privilege of playing my own arrangements and Breton-influenced compositions alongside one of my musical heroes, guitarist Soig Siberil. I also experienced the kick of having a group of dancers launch into an impromptu "en dro" while I played a fingerstyle guitar medley.

Over the years I have continued to play Breton music when I get the chance to play with other players who are familiar with the style and the repertoire. Among them special mention must go to Jeremiah McLane, one of my oldest musical compatriots, who's always up for a tune and who knows a lot of good ones. I hope that in assembling this modest collection, American players like myself who are looking for players to play with and tunes to play will have another resource to draw on. These settings are deliberately sparse, and keyed to fall comfortably on the fiddle, with chords suggested for most of them. They should sound good with the same type of instrumentation one would find at a good Irish session.

One of the most important things to do is to listen to players who play Breton music, preferably the ones from Brittany! To that end I have chosen mostly traditional tunes that have been recorded, and have provided the notes as to where to find the versions. To my ears some of the most interesting sounds are the four and five-piece "fest-noz" groups, usually featuring bombarde, fiddle, accordion or flute backed by guitar, bouzouki, or bass, in varying combos. The majority of the tunes come from recordings of these groups. Of course the modern Breton folk music scene is extremely diverse and vibrant, and you can find all sorts of different variations of the traditional (as well as not so traditional) sounds. I wish you happy listening and playing, and hope this music entrances you in the same way it still does me.

Breton Dance Tunes

The tunes in this collection are all traditional dance tunes, similar in many ways to the jigs and reels that make up the repertoire of most "fiddle tune" traditions, such as Irish, New England, old-time, and so on. There are a number of points of interest when comparing Breton dance tunes to tunes from these other traditions.

To begin, one must look at the dances which accompany the tunes (or is that backwards?). A key point, for here the Breton repertoire is more like the New England contradance repertoire than the Irish session repertoire, in that their primary use is in actual dance settings. The number of different dances in Brittany is quite large, especially if one takes into account regional varieties of some of the more popular dances (the *gavotte*, for example). The dances can be roughly grouped into three large categories. The oldest are the chain or circle dances, such as the *gavotte*, *en dro*, *hanter dro*, and *laridé*, and it is these which make up the majority of tunes in this book. The second category includes dances that have steps influenced by quadrilles and contredanses, including the *derobée* and the *pach-pi*. The third category is couples dances such as the *polka* and the *schottische*.

Many of the older tunes are frequently danced in three and four-part suites, where the faster steps are interspersed with slower, restful moments. These provide the dancers with a respite, and also offer the musicians an opportunity for more personal expression and variation. The *Tamm Kreiz* in this book is from a gavotte suite, and the *baleu* in 6/8 comes from a rond suite. It would be especially important to listen to a suite in its entirety, to really hear the rhythmic subtleties that are not easily conveyed by conventional notation.

Another important distinction within Brittany itself is the difference between the western Breton-speaking part (Basse-Bretagne, or Breizh-Izel), and the eastern part (Haute-Bretagne, or Breizh-Uhel), speaking primarily French or a French dialect called Gallo. The traditional repertoires of these areas are very different, and most of the tunes in this book come from the westernmost areas, with the exception of the Ronds. The vast majority of my time in Brittany has been spent in the west, and this fact seems to be reflected in my CD collection as well!

Most of the tunes in this book used either bombarde or fiddle as the main point of reference for the basic version. With fiddle, I have tended to transcribe them in the same key they were played. Bombardes, however, are most often in the key of B-flat, although many players today use bombardes made in a number of different keys. Many fiddlers who play with B-flat bombardes tune their fiddles up a half-step, placing the scale of B-flat into an A fingering. This will account for the number of A and B minor tunes. I also tried to provide variety, sometimes moving the tunes into a key I felt was particularly nice for them. A lot of the tunes are short, and I have tried to pair them on the page with another tune that would sound good in medley.

Many of these melodies can be found used for several different dances, depending on the tempo and rhythmic feel used. As tempos vary quite a bit, depending on the region, the players, and the dancers, I have not given dance tempo indications. I would hope that players would listen to recordings (and live players, too, if possible!) in order to arrive at a good tempo. It's also probably worth noting that most players here in the US will probably not be playing for dancing, bur rather for listening and for pleasure. However, all players of dance music from any tradition would do well to learn some of the dance steps that go with the dance tunes.

I have also tried to provide a basic, sparsely-ornamented version of the tune. As in most Celtic music, melodic ornamentation in Breton music is highly developed, and is considered a mark of a more accomplished player. Most tune players I know tend to prefer a spare version to which they can add their own ornaments. The grace notes and triplets and such would be similar to other piping and fiddle traditions, and again, one would hope that listening and good taste would help to achieve satisfactory results.

The chords, as is typical with tune accompaniment, are a personal choice and open to discussion, revision, and interpretation. I have given what I would consider a basic version to start with, and would encourage accompanists to try to develop rhythmic and chordal variety as the tunes progress. Brittany is loaded with wonderful players of all instruments, and as a guitarist I am a huge admirer of Soig Siberil and Gilles LeBigot, who are both remarkable accompanists and well worth a listen.

Letter from Brittany

The following article is reprinted from the February 1996 issue of *Acoustic Guitar* magazine. It was an "AG Letter" about traditional Breton music from the guitar perspective, and was an outgrowth of a two week trip around westernmost Brittany in the spring of 1995.

Dear Musicians,

At Europe's western fringe lies Brittany, a Celtic region contained within the greater Gallic hexagon. Finistere, quite literally the "end of the earth" (*fin de terre*), is at the westernmost edge of this ancient province, a land of savage and beautiful coastline, of graceful cities such as Quimper, of fishermen and farmers. It's also a land with a rich heritage of traditional music and dance, which remains vibrant today. I'm spending a couple of weeks in Finistere, supported in part by a grant from Arts International, to learn more about the traditional dance music of Brittany and meet some of the region's outstanding guitarists.

Throughout Brittany there is a strong sense of pride in the Breton heritage. This pride has not come easily; the Bretons have had to overcome the influence of hundreds of years of French efforts to undermine traditional Breton culture and language. Today there is more official tolerance from Paris, and many children attend bilingual schools. Yet Breton speakers remain a minority, and music is perhaps the strongest contemporary link with the region's Celtic heritage.

The folk music of Brittany is based around two traditions. There's a rich vocal tradition of many types of songs, including dramatic medieval ballads called *gwerz*, all sung in the Breton language. There's an equally strong instrumental tradition based around a pair of instruments that are typically played together: the *bombarde*, which is an earlier form of the oboe, and a one-droned bagpipe called the *biniou*. When paired, these instruments (and their respective players) form a *couple de sonneurs*. The *bombarde* and *biniou* play the dance music of Brittany – the *gavottes, en dros, laridés, plinns,* and *ronds*. There's also crossover between the repertoires, as singers frequently sing in pairs or small groups for dances in a style known as *kan ha diskan*, while *sonneurs* may play instrumental versions of *gwerz* airs.

Breton dances, or *fest-noz*, are one of the primary spots for young and old alike to hear these traditional styles. Once a purely local event in a rural, agrarian society, the *fest-noz* now draw a wider range of people. The Festival En Arwen celebrated its tenth anniversary in the spring of 1995 with a grand *fest-noz* that drew some 13,000 people, many of them in their teens and 20s.

One of the best nights of music and dance that I've experienced was at a *fest-noz* in the little town of Huelgoat in central Brittany. An area of Brittany that still retains much of what is left of traditional rural life, this is also the land of the *gavotte*. People here are very enamored of this dance.

The little dance hall was set up with a small stage for the musicians and singers, a well-worn wooden floor for the dancers, and a small bar dispensing beer, cider, wine, and soft drinks. The music for the evening was provided by two pairs of *sonneurs*, the group Storvan, and two pairs of *kan ha diskan* singers.

The music began as the bombarde and fiddle traded musical phrases in a relaxed, rhythmically free manner, calling people to the dance. Soon the bombarde jumped in on the end of the fiddle's phrase, the tempo picked up, the dancers joined in, and we were off, arms linked together as we stepped and hopped around the hall.

Gavottes were indeed plentiful, and I was in the midst of a long chain when an older fellow jumped into the center of the circle. The crowd cheered as he ran across the floor and took the hand of one of the younger singers, Annie Ebrel. He escorted her into the middle of the floor, and they executed some fancy steps together, his red face beaming. They finished with four little kisses on the cheeks, and the man stepped back into the crowd.

I discovered with a mixture of pleasure and horror that my hand was being taken by the singer, and I was being led into the circle to execute (or rather, massacre) some fancy steps that I had never quite picked up in my years of contra-dancing. I managed to hop about in a reasonable imitation of what she was doing, and I remembered the kisses. She smiled and stepped back into the line. I smiled and stepped back into the line, too, which elicited howls of laughter and protest. Back I went into the circle to choose a partner for another series of funny little hops and funny little kisses, before I was finally allowed to melt back into the group of dancers.

Although Breton traditional music is flourishing today, in the first half of the 20th century, the tradition seemed to be dying out. Several factors contributed to its revitalization, including the evolution of the *fest-noz* from a local gathering to a more modern form of folk entertainment, and the efforts of organizations such as *Bodadeg Ar Sonerion*, which helped a new generation learn to play the bombarde and bagpipes. Perhaps the most important influence was the music of *sonneur*, harper, and folk guru Alan Stivell.

Dan Ar Braz was Stivell's guitarist for many years, and played on most of his classic recordings from the late '60s and early '70s before embarking on a solo career of his own. Coming from a rock background, Ar Braz credits Stivell with exposing him to Breton music and Celtic music in general. "It was a return to their roots," he says of the young people who flocked to hear Stivell's mix of traditional folk and rock. "It was a worldwide movement, where there was music but also poetry, political action, environmentalism. And it was a movement for which Stivell was very responsible, because it was he who brought Brittany to Paris."

Gilles LeBigot, one of Brittany's finest guitarists, began with a background in folk and rock and with strong interests in players such as John Renbourn and Doc Watson. "One day, when I was 17 years old," he remembers, "I discovered Alan Stivell. He's someone who inspired an enormous amount of today's musicians to play Breton music." For young Breton musicians, Breton music was not merely another music, like blues or rock; it was *their* music, a part of their heritage that was suddenly being revealed to them.

Soig Siberil is another guitarist who was a convert to Breton music. As a Breton growing up in Paris, he started out playing American folk and bluegrass. "When I was 20," he recalls, "I came to live in Brittany. I began to go to the *fest-noz,* and it was a total shock. The American music was fine, but it was not my music. Breton music is my music. I completely gave up playing American music to get deeper into playing Breton music."

Although the guitar was not part of the Breton traditional music scene before the '60s, it was readily adopted by this new generation of musicians and has become standard in the groups that are now the dominant force at the *fest-noz.* Usually featuring bombarde, and sometimes a *biniou* or singers, the groups usually add other instruments such as fiddle, accordion, flute, guitar, and bouzouki to the mix, mellowing the raucous sound of the bombarde. Many of these instruments were borrowed from their Celtic kin, the Irish, whose music has been very popular and influential in Brittany since the '70s.

"The first time I heard open-tuned guitar," says Siberil, "was from the first Bothy Band record, in '74 or '75. And that was really a revelation. I had no idea how it worked. Afterwards, I had the chance to meet Michael O'Domnhaill; he was touring in Brittany, and he explained to me the idea of open tuning. I told myself, that's what we need for Breton music. So I've worked in this area, although the style of accompaniment is quite different compared to Irish music."

Gilles LeBigot's experience was similar to Siberil's; both now play exclusively in DADGAD tuning. "When I began with this tuning," says LeBigot, "I soon learned how to play Irish music. I was often with Jean-Michel Veillon; he plays lots of jigs and reels, and he also was adapting Breton music to the Irish flute. One could say that this work was being done in common on many different instruments. At the same time that guitarists like Soig and myself were adapting accompaniments to Breton music, flutists like Jean-Michel were adapting Breton music to the flute, and many violin players who were well-versed in Irish music were adapting Breton tunes to the fiddle. So this created groups like Galorn, Pennou Skoulm, and Kornog, among others." Both Siberil and LeBigot played in Kornog, undoubtedly one of the best groups to come out of Brittany and one of a handful of groups that helped to redefine the sound of Breton music.

"We tried, with Kornog, to present Breton music in somewhat the same manner that Irish groups were presenting Irish music," says Siberil, "with bouzouki and guitar accompaniment, and soloists like Jean-Michel and Christian (LeMaitre, on fiddle). So it was with groups like these that the 'new wave' of Breton music began. There had been other groups with more of a folk/rock sound, but not groups with a totally acoustic sound. That began with Pennou Skoulm, and it continued. There was an evolution, and now there are lots of groups playing in this style."

Despite the strong Irish influence, Breton music remains very different from Irish music, perhaps deceptively so. "Breton music is very modal," says LeBigot. "There are Breton tunes where there are only four notes. When you accompany this music, you can't be thinking major scale or minor scale; you have to think differently. The open tuning permits you, while keeping a drone, to have chords that sound good and that don't have a third."

"I find Breton music more difficult than Irish music," confesses Siberil. "Not technically, because with *gavottes* and *en dros* there are fairly simple melodic phrases. The difficulty is in the style, in accompaniment as well as on a melodic level. Everything I've tried to do on the guitar comes from having listened to *sonneurs* and singers, and from having danced it. I find that for Breton music, it's also important to know the dances to really play it well."

Guitar in Brittany is not, of course, limited to traditional music. While I was there I was able to take part in the "Nuit des Guitares Oceanes" (Night of the Oceanic Guitars!), a concert at the cultural center at Benodet, a beautiful little coastal resort town just south of Quimper. The event was organized by Pierre Cabon, a guitarist from Benodet who now teaches music in Paris, and Thierry Guillo, the director of the cultural center. I had been attracted by Soig Siberil's name on the poster, but the music was far from strictly traditional or folk. Classical styles were well-represented by Cabon and Tom O'Farrel, a genial Irishman now living in Brittany, whose repertoire mixed modern classical with his own classically-flavored arrangements of Irish dance tunes and harp music. Siberil's solo presentation showed his skill at adapting Breton dance tunes and slow airs to the guitar, as well as his own traditionally-based compositions. A trio of guitarists led by the inimitable Jacques Pellen finished up the night with a mixture of jazz standards and originals. Both Dan Ar Braz and Siberil spoke admiringly of Pellen as someone who possesses formidable technique yet always plays with taste and musicality — qualities that were in evidence throughout his set.

In two weeks of traveling around Finistere with a guitar slung over my shoulder, I was struck by how integral music is to the culture. Several nights turned into impromptu jam sessions, such as the one at the Eden Bar in Quimper. In my quest to learn more about Breton music, I was told to go and see the owner, Christian Lautredou, a drummer who had played with the pipe band Bagad Kemper. As it turned out, he's also a pretty decent fingerstyle guitar player.

Bars and cafés are an integral part of daily life in Brittany and serve as community gathering spots. During the Festival En Arwen in Cleguerec, a town of several thousand, the half-dozen or so bars and cafés were overflowing with musicians and revelers, with jam sessions ranging from Breton to Irish to French. I ended up at a late-night Irish session with Christian LeMaitre, a wonderful fiddle player equally adept at Irish and Breton music.

"It's true that this place inspires painters, poets, and musicians," guitarist Dan Ar Braz said as we sat at another café in the heart of Quimper. "The only difference is that some draw their inspiration from traditional music. I've never tried to make music that was absolutely Celtic. I search for musical colors that express a spirit, a way of life, and a way that is a part of me." This spirit is beautifully expressed in *Heritage des Celtes*, his most recent album, a collaboration between Breton, Irish, Scottish, and Welsh musicians for Quimper's *Festival de la Cornouaille* in 1993. The music contains elements of all these Celtic traditions, yet maintains a feel and a mood that seem quintessentially Breton.

Ar Braz added, "The greatest compliment I got was from an Italian fan. 'I know your music,' he said. 'I came to Brittany, and I saw why you've written this music.' It's because I come from here. I speak often about the sea, about the region, because I was born here, and I really feel at home here. So it's all these little things that have nothing to do with musical technique. Now I'm aware of it, but at the time I was simply trying to touch the countryside, the light, the people, memories, childhood – all the little things of life."

It's those little things that linger in my memory as well.

Kenavo (au revoir),

David Surette (1996)

From Acoustic Guitar, *February 1996, Issue No. 38.*
© 1996 String Letter Publishing. All rights reserved.
For more information on Acoustic Guitar,
contact String Letter Publishing, PO Box 767, San Anselmo, CA 94979;
(415) 485-6946; fax (415) 485-0831; www.stringletter.com.

14

Fest Breizh

Gavotte

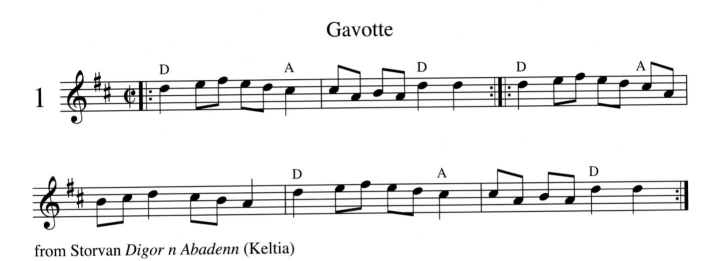

from Storvan *Digor n Abadenn* (Keltia)

Gavotte de Scrignac

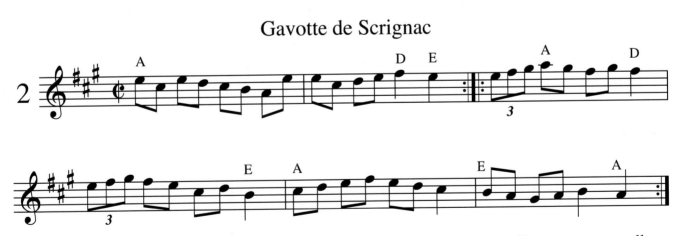

from Gerald Trimble *First Flight* (Green Linnet). Scrignac is a Breton town. Breton tunes usually have no names, other than the town or region they are from and the tune type.

Gavotte

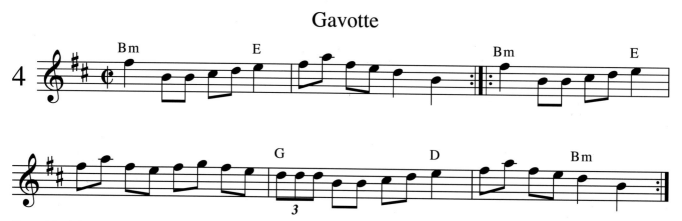

from Padrig Sicard *A Way for Brittany — Traditional Breton Music* (Escalibur/Coop Breizh). Some of the tunes in this medley were also recorded by fiddler Kevin Burke on *Promenade*.

Gavotte

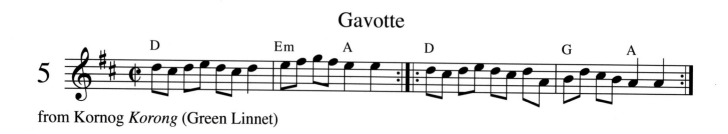

from Padrig Sicard *A Way for Brittany — Traditional Breton Music* (Escalibur/Coop Breizh). Some of the tunes in this medley were also recorded by fiddler Kevin Burke on *Promenade*.

Gavotte

from Kornog *Korong* (Green Linnet)

Gavotte

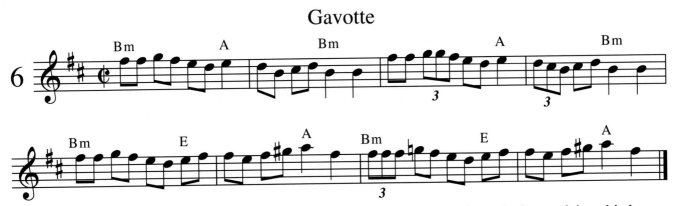

Both this and the next gavotte were learned from guitarist Gilles LeBigot, during a visit to his home in Douarnenez. Thanks, Gilles. He is also the composer of the very popular waltz, *Soir et Matin*.

Gavotte

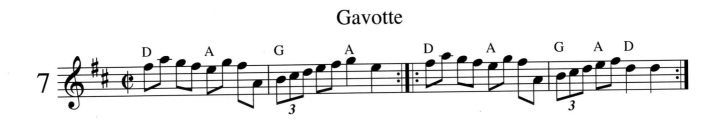

Gavotte Montagnes

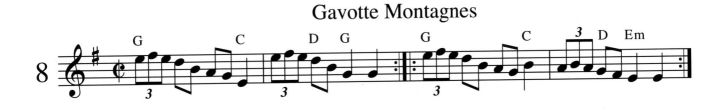

Gavotte Montagnes

both from the band Skolvan on the *Dans Musique a danser de Bretagne* (Adipho) compilation. The mountains or montagnes of the titles are the Montagnes Noires, or Black Mountains, of central Brittany. This is an area where the gavotte is very popular.

Gavotte des Montagnes

from Dremmwel *Heol-loar* (Coop Breizh)

Gavotte Montagne

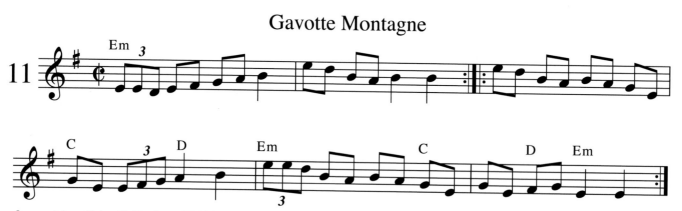

from Alan Stivell *Reflet*s (Editions Keltia III). This tune is also part of a great guitar medley that leads off Pierre Bensusan's first album, *Pres de Paris*.

Gavotte Pourlet

from Alan Stivell *E Langonned* (Editions Keltia III). The word *Pourlet* refers to another localized variation on the typical gavotte.

Gavotte de Huelgoat

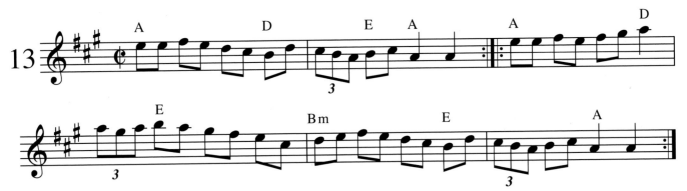

from Kornog *4* (An naer) Huelgoat is a lovely little town in central Brittany.

Gavotte des Montagnes

from Tud *Deus Kerne* (Escalibur/Coop Breizh)

Gavotte des Montagnes

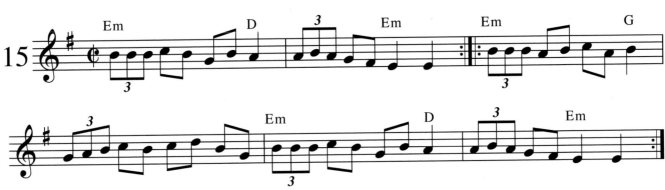

from Tud *Deus Kerne* (Escalibur/Coop Breizh)

Tamm Kreiz (suite des Gavottes Montagnes)

from Storvan *Digor n Abadenn* (Keltia). This tune is for the bal section of a gavotte suite. The first phrase is played freely as the chain moves a few steps, then the second phrase is in time as people perform the footwork of the dance in place.

Gavotte des Montagnes

from Storvan *Digor n Abadenn* (Keltia)

Dans Fisel

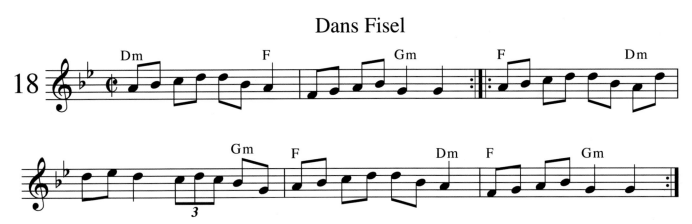

from Barzaz *An den kozh dall* (Keltia). This tune is also found in B minor on Christian LeMaitre's *Ballade a l'hôtesse* (Escalibur/Coop Breizh), and is printed in B minor also. The tunes for the dans fisel are very similar to gavottes.

Dans Fisel (B minor version)

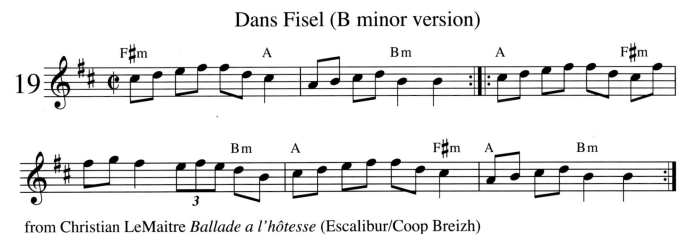

from Christian LeMaitre *Ballade a l'hôtesse* (Escalibur/Coop Breizh)

Dans Fisel

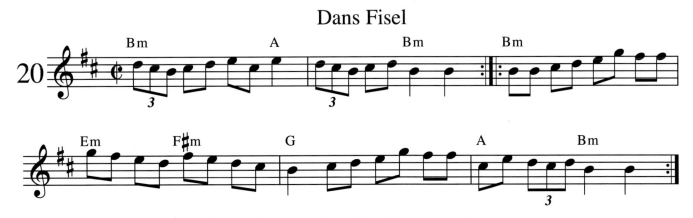

from Christian LeMaitre *Ballade a l'hôtesse* (Escalibu/Coop Breizh)

22

En Dro Nevez

21

from Alan Stivell *Chemins de Terre* (Editions Keltia III)

En Dro

22

from *Recueil d'airs a danser: pays vannetais* by Padrig Sicard (Dastum)

Kas Ha Barh (En Dro)

from Storvan *Digor n Abadenn* (Keltia). The kas ha barh is a couple dance version of the en dro, and the tunes are the same.

En Dro

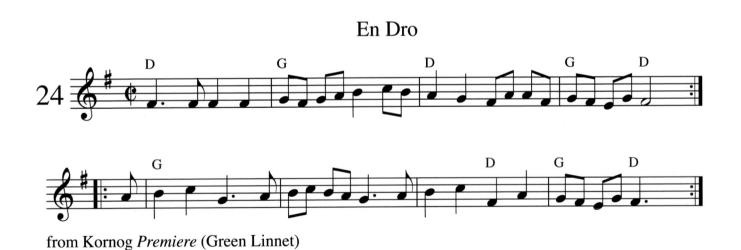

from Kornog *Premiere* (Green Linnet)

En Dro

25

from Padrig Sicard *A Way for Brittany Traditional Breton Music* (Escalibur/Coop Breizh)

En Dro

26

from *Recueil d'airs a danser: pays vannetais* by Padrig Sicard (Dastum). I learned this tune from the Sicard book and taught it to California guitarist Steve Baughman; we recorded it together on his CD *The Angel's Portion* (Solid Air Records).

En Dro

I learned both these tunes from West Coast hurdy-gurdy player Chris Wright, who plays mostly traditional French tunes. Thanks, Chris.

En Dro

Hanter Dro

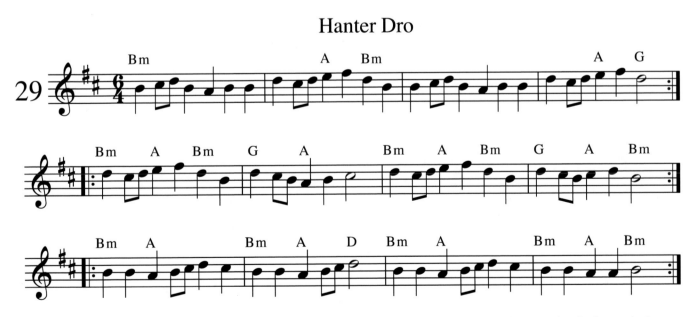

also from Chris Wright. The 6/4 rhythm is more like 4/4 than 6/8, in that the emphasis is on 1, 3, and 5, as opposed to 1 and 4.

Hanter Dro

from Storvan *An deiziou kaer* (Keltia)

Hanter Dro

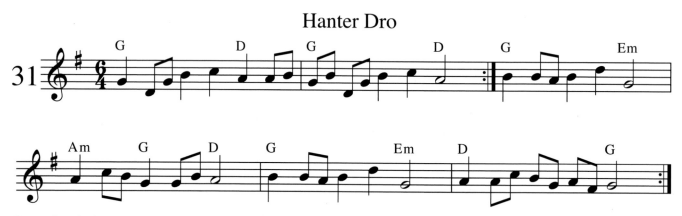

from Strakal on the *Dans Musique a danser de Bretagne* (Adipho) compilation

Marche de Glomel

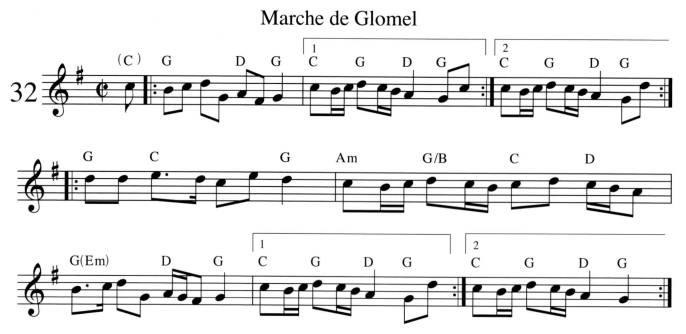

from Pennou Skoulm *Fest Noz* (Escalibur/Coop Breizh). This tune has also been a favorite of Celtic guitarists, recorded by Tony McManus as well as on my *Trip to Kemper* CD.

Laridé

Both these tunes are from Storvan on the *Dans Musique a danser de Bretagne* (Adipho) compilation, and are also found on my *Northern Roots* CD.

Laridé

28

Laridé

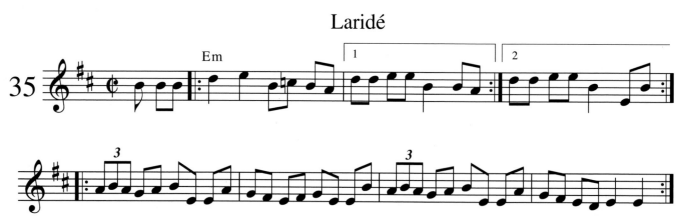

This tune and the one that follows are from Skolvan on the *Dans Musique a danser de Bretagne* (Adipho) compilation, and are also found on *Trip to Kemper*. They were also recorded by Gilles LeBigot and Serge Desaunay on *Tunes for America*, a self-produced and out of print cassette that made the rounds of the American dance musician's community in the late 80s.

Laridé

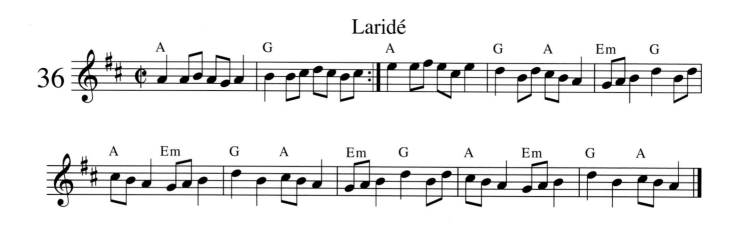

Pach-pi Kozh

from Alan Stivell *Live in Dublin* (Editions Keltia III)

Laridé

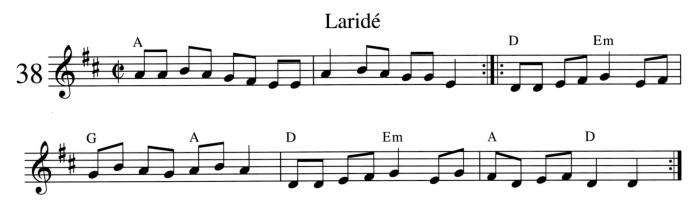

38

from from *Recueil d'airs a danser: pays vannetais* by Padrig Sicard (Dastum); also on *Trip to Kemper.*

Veuze Tune

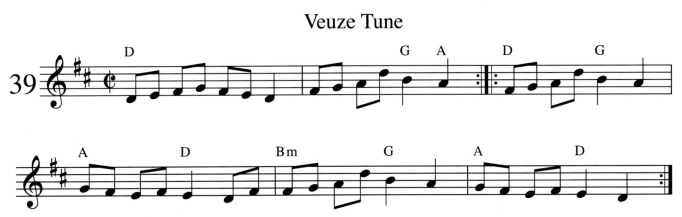

39

from Various Artists *A Celebration of Bagpipes* (Keltia); also on *Trip to Kemper.* A veuze is a particular type of bagpipe from the Nantes region.

Laridé

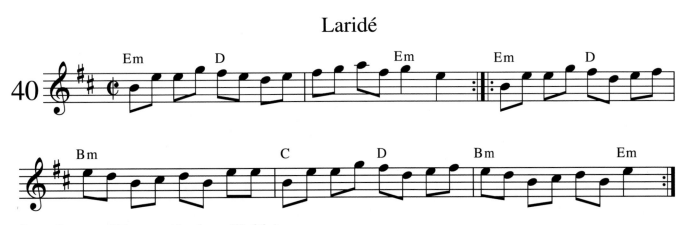

40

from Storvan *Digor n Abadenn* (Keltia)

Laridé

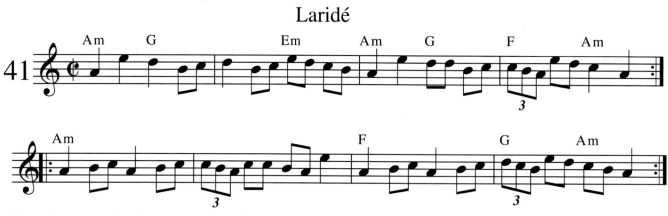

from Dremmwel *Glazik* (Escalibur/Coop Breizh)

Laridé

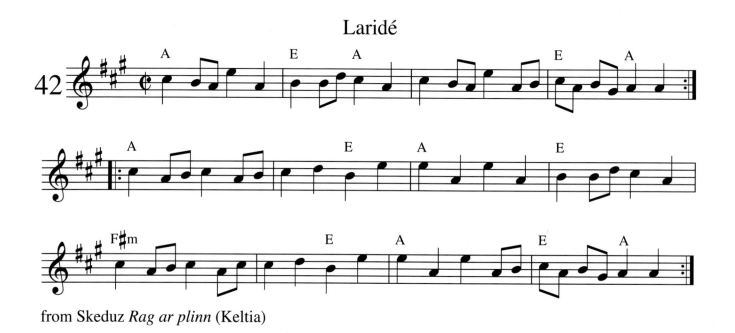

from Skeduz *Rag ar plinn* (Keltia)

Laridé (6 count)

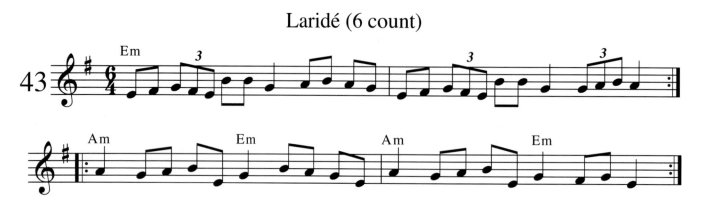

from Strobinell *An aotrou liskildri* (Keltia)

Rond de Loudeac

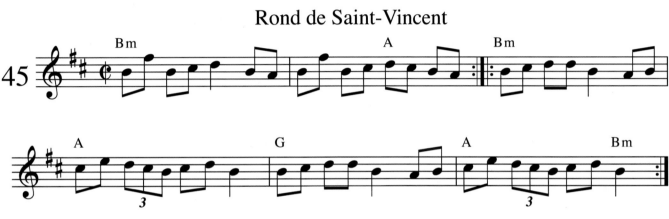

44

from Jean Baron and Christian Anneix *Dansal e Breiz* (Keltia)

Rond de Saint-Vincent

45

from Skeduz *Rag ar plinn* (Keltia)

Rond de Loudeac

46

from a recording of a pub session I made during the *Festival En Arwen* in Cleguerec in the spring of '95

Rond de Loudeac

from Jean Baron and Christian Anneix *Dansal e Breiz* (Keltia)

Baleu from Loudeac

from Kornog *Premiere* (Green Linnet)

Enez Sant Lorans

from Christian LeMaitre *Ballade a l'hôtesse* (Escalibur/Coop Breizh). Both this tune and Son Ar Rost were composed by bagpiper Herri Leon, an important figure in the revival of Breton traditional music in the 1950s.

Son Ar Rost

from Kornog *Premiere* (Green Linnet)
Translated as "The Roast Tune", this tune would form part of the music played at a traditional Breton wedding. In this case, it would accompany the presentation of the roast meat course.

Derobée de Guingamp

51

from Alan Stivell *Live in Dublin* (Editions Keltia III)

Discography

Jean Baron and Christian Anneix *Dansal e Breiz* (Keltia)
Barzaz *An den kozh dall* (Keltia)
Steve Baughman *The Angel's Portion* (Solid Air Records)
Serge Desaunay/Gilles LeBigot *Tunes for America* (self-produced, out of print)
Dremmwel *Glazik* (Escalibur/Coop Breizh)
Dremmwel *Heol-loar* (Coop Breizh)
Kornog *Korong* (Green Linnet)
Kornog *Premiere* (Green Linnet)
Kornog *4* (An naer)
Christian LeMaitre *Ballade à l'hôtesse* (Escalibur/Coop Breizh)
Pennou Skoulm *Fest Noz* (Escalibur/Coop Breizh)
Padrig Sicard *A Way for Brittany – Traditional Breton Music* (Escalibur/Coop Breizh)
Skeduz *Rag ar plinn* (Keltia)
Alan Stivell *Reflets* (Editions Keltia III)
Alan Stivell *Live in Dublin* ((Editions Keltia III)
Alan Stivell *Chemins de Terre* (Editions Keltia III)
Alan Stivell *E Langonned* (Editions Keltia III)
Storvan *Digor n Abadenn* (Keltia)
Storvan *An deiziou kaer* (Keltia)
Strobinell *An aotrou liskildri* (Keltia)
Gerald Trimble *First Flight* (Green Linnet)
Tud *Deus Kerne* (Escalibur/Coop Breizh)
Various Artists *A Celebration of Bagpipes* (Keltia)
Various Artists *Dans – Musique à danser de Bretagne* (Adipho)

Bibliography

La Musique Bretonne by Roland Becker and Laure Le Gurun (Coop Breizh)
Recueil d'airs a danser: pays vannetais by Padrig Sicard (Dastum)
Guide to Breton Music by Lois Kuter
(available online at www.breizh.net/icdbl/saozg/index.htm *click on the* "music" *link)*

Further Resources

Coop Breizh (CDs, books; production, distribution)
Kerangwenn
29540 Spezed
Telephone: (33) 02 98 93 83 14
web site: http//www.coop-breizh.fr

Dastum (CDs, books; production, distribution, archives and research)
16 rue de la Santé
35000 Rennes
Telephone: (33) 02 99 30 91 00
E-mail: dastum@wanadoo.fr
Web site: http://www.dastum.net

Keltia Musique (CDs, books; production, distribution)
1 place au Beurre
29000 Quimper
Telephone : (33) 02 98 95 45 82
E-mail: mailto:keltia@eurobretagne
Web site: http://www.keltiamusique.com

International Committee for the Defense of the Breton Language (ICDBL)

This group, and especially Dr. Lois Kuter, has been enormously helpful to me over the years in planning trips to Brittany. They are passionate and knowledgeable about the culture, and music is a big part of their focus, in addition to language. They publish a quarterly magazine called *Bro Nevez* (in English); also check out their excellent website at www.breizh.net/icdbl/saozg/index.htm, which contains a great "Guide to Breton Music" as well as a large links section.

David Surette also has three solo instrumental albums available, each of which contans Breton and Breton-influenced material, as well as a book of Celtic guitar arrangements. Additional information on all of these is available at :
www.BurkeSurette.com

———————

"Surette has distinguished himself among North American Celtic guitarists by his use of Breton and French materials....His technique is impeccable, and his touch and phrasing are immediately recognizable."

Acoustic Guitar

———————

"A brilliant soloist, in the acoustic Celtic fingerstyle genre..."

Trad Magazine (France)

———————

"...le type de synthese a laquelle se livere David Surete est plutôt singulier...il faut dire qu'il commence a bien connaitre la Bretagne."

Ar Men (Brittany, France)

———————

"Surett's playing is always inventive, and sets a new standard for traditional instrumentalists."

Sing Out

UNIQUELY INTERESTING MUSIC!